ANCHOR BOOKS

LOOKING FORWARD
LOOKING BACK

First published in Great Britain in 1994 by
ANCHOR BOOKS
1-2 Wainman Road, Woodston,
Peterborough, PE2 7BU

Foreword

Looking Forward Looking Back is a collection of futuristic and nostalgic poetry, detailing the perceived visions of life in the future in comparison to the life and times of days gone by.

Included are poems portraying fears and hopes for the future, and also poems which look back to the lifestyle of previous years.

I have chosen the poems which show understanding and depth, and those that enable us to paint a picture in our minds of the particular age.

I hope that you will enjoy this collection as much as I have compiling it.

Michelle Abbott
Editor

Contents

Looking Forward . . .

Universal Wanderer

It is difficult being a universal wanderer,
For too few understand
What it is like to belong to no woman or any man.
It is tough being a universal wanderer,
Loving every land that you pass through,
And recognising every living thing as being a part of you.
And although there is no land that you own, every one is your home,
It is not easy being a universal wanderer for too few know or
understand the worth,
Of having an empathy with the Mother Earth.
Or know how it feels to let your spirit fly wild and free,
Soaring across the universe and seeking out new galaxies.
It is not an easy life being an universal wanderer,
Dreaming dreams that have no end,
Hoping mankind has at last become his friend,
That all men do finally united stand, at last there truly is a
brotherhood of man.
Yes, it is difficult being a universal wanderer,
But I guess I am lucky, in fact I know that I am,
Blessed to be born a universal wanderer,
Rather than a cybernetic man or woman.

Maureen M Anderson

Fiery Chariots

One summer's day I little thought
   What wealth to me, this show had brought
Driving along this stony lane I sped -
   My eyes up heavenward then led -

Six fiery chariots each separate course
   No smoke or fumes or regular force
Zig zag paths from heavens to hover
   Silent motion, spinning top cover -

I stopped with field glasses to fully gaze
   On six fiery chariots at each phrase -
Spinning, lit up of saucer like shape
   Above house tops, trees lightening escape!

Standing spell bound, watching aghast!
   Never seen at sea or ship or on mast
Such lightening speed, a flash! then gone
   Drawn to a larger cigar shaped one!

Some as they came - on speed zig zag path
   At speed of lightening - no after math!
Just total amazement of what I saw -
   Though unbelievable, noise shout evermore!

Police on duty, pilots, responsible folk,
   Has been claimed by many others I joke,
Spoken to - seeing is believing, I say
   I know what I saw there that day!

Geoffrey Wilyman

Science Sense

When I lift up my head what do I see?
Letting my mind and eyes roam free,
Knowing we are not the only planet in the universe of sea
What knowledge there could be for all man to know and see.
There must be other life out there God made not just you and me
How they survive what would their earth be
Do they have wars, kill each other like you and me
Is there so much hate out there that peace cannot be.
Like on TV would it be like Star Trek and Dr Who
What would you think us civilised so called man would do?
Man is a destroyer of what he does not know or understand
Perhaps given a chance they could out there help us save this planet
Bring back peace and fellowship to our human man.
Why on TV do they show domination and fear?
Let our hand of friendship go out across skies clear,
With crop circles and spaceships what are they trying to say to us
We are advanced to you let us help you don't cause a fuss
Come to our planets come and see what generations of peace
                                                                could be,
No need to starve or be ill cure with love no need for pill
Science should be to cure not to kill it should be for good not ill
Like they show us on our screen would they be ugly and mean.
Our clothes like our body is just a covering outside shell
What's inside if we let out is beautiful full of love a binding spell
No matter two heads, three arms, blue or any colour crest
Let man rule with his heart not head and life will be it's best.
I expect they have learned what earthman is striving to know
Let hand in hand to their planets with them we should go
With knowledge, love and peace all planets of the universe
                                                                power will increase.

Daphne Margaret Pook

3

Intergalactic Job Application

Dear Red Dwarf Crew, I'd like to apply
For a job with you as you travel the sky.
I'd take over the chores and leave you free
To conquer space in time for tea.

I could help with repairs and give Kryten a break,
I could plait Lister's hair and make chocolate cake;
I could be nice to Rimmer and keep Cat well dressed,
And my cooking's delicious - you'd be most impressed.

I could do all the housework and tidy your bug,
Red Dwarf would soon become cosy and snug.
From the mess you're in now it's plain to see
That what you all need is a Mum like me.

Linda Kingston

Star Trek

There they go across the sky
Captain Kirk and the good ship Enterprise,
Holding steady the swift going ship
Giving commands amid ship.
Now what can we see nothing normally
Let us beam down and see,
Active stations hands on the buttons
Mr Spock gives the go ahead
One, two, three.

G Jones

Stretching the Imagination!

When once up on a time
always began a story line,
imagination travelled familiar terrain,
through forests, deserts, mountains, plain.
Coloured pictures visually aid perception
pop up cut outs gave extra inspection.

Then even police boxes of blue
were not so unusual to view.
But, we entered the age of space
a new encounter for the human race.
Television gave us a different medium
transporting rapidly without tedium.

Opening up new visual dimensions
assailing minds wider comprehensions.
It was a doctor of many identities, *Who,*
became the vehicle of adventures new.
The police box to a tardis changed
inside mysterious new technology arranged.

Thus moving forwards; backwards through time
new licence was given to a story line.
So silver darlek glided, robotically driven,
to exterminate : were their deadly orders given.
Next travelling the star ship Enterprise
through new galaxies and uncharted skies.

Beyond Andromeda and ever on and on
through time warps, holes, falling, gone.
So star wars vivid lasered beams
ripped conventional thought to the seams.
Can we assimilate future psychedelic sights,
new multi dimensional projections, fancies, flights?

H D Hensman

The Final Frontier

Steadily cruising through outer space,
Furthering the aims of the human race,
Sweeping along the galactic skies,
United States Starship, The Enterprise.

Five hundred crew continually work,
To serve their Captain, James T Kirk,
As their first class efforts make them strive,
To increase the speed into top warp drive.

Avoiding black holes and asteroids,
Exploring stars and planetoids,
Or nova and destructive rock,
That task belongs to Mr Spock.

To Scottie, the Enterprise engineer,
With lithium crystal's, naught to fear,
As Dr McCoy with technical ease,
Protects the crew from every disease.

It's possible to move like the crack of doom,
From the ship's itinerant transporter room,
And beaming up occurs on the double,
If the team below is in serious trouble.

The prime objective, to preserve all life,
In every planet regardless of strife,
To interfere, one must not decree,
But establish a firm democracy.

A subject of the Federation,
The ship supports each terrain nation,
To boldly go in peace or war,
Where no man has ever gone before!

Stan Mason

Calling Outer Space

Is there something out there?
A Dr Who or a Captain Black?
What about ET?
What do you think of that?
Could this possibly have been true
Can you accept it? It's up to you.
Oh no! Don't expect me to tell you what's right
You will have to depend on your own insight
Into these strange phenomenal things
Like *flying saucers* and *cornfield rings.*
Are we the one and only race
Inhabiting a place in this mysterious
Universal galaxy of sun, moon and stars?
We know about Venus, Pluto and Mars.
What of these aliens - do they exist?
Or have they been seen through an imaginary *mist?*

Evelyn A Evans

The Twilight Zone

I stepped into the Twilight Zone
one dark and ghostly night
What I seen and felt there
gave me such a fright.

All my nightmares were combined
alone in this dark place
The Twilight Zone was somewhere
somewhere, in Outer Space.

I screamed for help and heard myself
so very far away
Aliens surrounded me
whispering, 'Here you'll stay.'

By chance I'd found this Twilight Zone
where no man wants to be
Caught in time, suspended
in Outer Space, that's me.

I stepped back from the Twilight Zone
the sun began to shine
The clock alarm had wakened me
brought me back *in time*.

Catherine Barrons

The Land of the Giants

It started as a trip through space
But now the crew feel out of place,
They crashed in a land of giants, you see
And now they're as tiny as can be.

A simple thing like a domestic pet
To the little people is such a threat,
Deep in the woods they hide away
And for now that's where they must stay.

While Steve works at repairing the ship,
The others go on a fact finding trip,
Fitsu as always complains all the way,
And as usual he'll have the last say.

Needles thread and thimbles too,
It's amazing what a little thought can do,
Objects the giants throw away,
Can always be used in some small way.

On this world they face dangers every day,
And there's a reward for their capture, the giants will pay,
It's work every day just to stay alive,
Because to return to earth they must survive.

Vivien Shore

Romantic Enterprise

Though Captain Kirk never would shirk, whatever he
                                        considered his duty,
He still has an eye, perhaps on the sly, for many an
                                        Earthling beauty;
Whilst Mr Spock, immune from shock, or any other
                                        human emotion,
With logic supreme, and face so serene, still fell for a female Vulcan.

Captain Picard, though outwardly hard, is inwardly soft as
                                        warm butter,
And strange to relate, despite his bald pate, warm words of
                                        love does he utter;
But strangest of all, to whom love should befall, is Data the
                                        android man
With the psychic girl, who put him in a whirl, by saying 'You can!
                                        You can!'
Now with all this romance, there isn't a chance, that our Star
                                        Trek ever will end,
The next generation, for our delectation, is a most peculiar blend
Of various races and even with traces, of Vulcan, Klingon and all,
With such Enterprise, can this song of the skies, once started,
                                        now go to the wall?

S J Short

11

A Moment in War of the Worlds

From out of the skies it came,
Bright and breathing out fire,
The lioness upon the plain awoke
At the spaceships hunger and desire.
Though no eye could focus upon its gleam,
Terror rang through everyone it seems.
The blasting of humans could be heard,
Far away,
And the tripods had every intention,
Of being here to stay.
Though screams and burning were everywhere,
I looked at this thing once and stared.
It was a beast,
There was no doubt,
Made of machinery,
Metal in and out.
I pointed my gun so feeble it seems,
But I shot!
Gave it all I'd got,
And the last thing I remember,
Was the gleam . . .

Mylene Bensley

Lister

Lister oh Lister, we think you're mega brill
Cruising through time and space
In Red Dwarf alongside your motley crew.

You pass through all the boundaries
Of reality it's often said
And disregarding general consensus
You ain't no smeg head.

Like a spacey new age traveller
In a league all of your own
Next to you cat and rimmer
Are second class drones.

Lister oh Lister, you give us such a thrill
We can't see you enough
We never get our fill
But for now it looks like we'll have to wait until . . .
The next series.
(Oh yes we will)

K Saul

Star Wars

Star Wars
Not meant to be
Historical
For you
Or me.
But fantasy
Of time
Of space
Of human beings
Of alien race.
A journey to
Fantasy land
Where Darth Vadar
Got out of hand.
Heroes, human
And robots.
Captured Princess.
You got the lot.
Daring Deeds
Princess rescued.
Battling vessels
Captains special.
Good o'er evil
Had to be.
Star Wars -
Heroes -
Victory.

June Rampton

14

Time and Relative Dimensions in Sitting Room!

Science fiction on TV
Comes through space
Direct to me.
And on through space
Goes Dr Who,
In the Tardis
Complete with crew.
Sarah and the Brigadier
Fighting aliens without fear;
Right across the galaxy,
Bringing happiness to me.
Up against the Cybermen
The Doctor triumphs once again.
The return of his old foe
The Master,
Makes the Doctor's brain go
Faster.
The Master plots the Earth's downfall,
But Dr Who can beat them all.
A final flourish ends my fears,
Then the Tardis disappears,
To turn up in another place
Through Time and Relative Dimensions in Space.

Michael Marshall

Who's a Hero

Travelling through time and space
He's out to save the human race,
The man they call the Doctor.
With his assistant, Jo or Ace,
He'll turn up at some troubled place,
Sometimes with a different face -
The man they call the Doctor.

Cyberman or Dalek,
Or that villain called the Master
He'll outwit the lot of them
He's cleverer and faster.

The powers that be commit the crime
Of killing off The Lord of Time,
Without a reason or a rhyme,
Or did they think he's past his prime
The man they call
The Doctor?

Ken Craven

The Golden Years

Sometimes I attempt to explain
My passion and delight,
For the silver warrior spaceships
That flash down through the night.
The fire power that they yield
Sends shivers 'long my spine,
The devastation of countless nations
Is as sweet as any wine.

And though I'm looked upon in sorrow,
'He'll grow out of it,' they explain,
I swear to H G Wells
That if I get older I'll never change.
For I have witnessed miracles,
I have seen the truth
That aged eyes don't recognise;
I'll always hang on to my youth.

Yes, I was there when Klaatu walked,
The Day that Earth Stood Still.
And I was there in darkest space,
When Ripley made the kill.
I patrolled the polar ice caps,
With The Thing from outer space.
And I survived When Worlds Collide,
Amen for the human race.

So hold your tongue and comment ye not,
Be gone with slights and slurs,
Take your place on the shores of space,
And remember the golden years.

Derek Rutherford

Peace in Space

Swirling and swaying and spinning around
The starships been hit and is nearing the ground,
To an unknown planet it's fleeing at speed
To stop for repairs, is the Enterprise need.

Bones is helping the injured on board
As items tumble down from where they were stored,
The starship is grounded, the panels are smashed
All the lights went out, when the Enterprise crashed.

The moans and the groans can be heard all around
Chekov is lying, face down on the ground
Sulu and Kelly scramble up very dazed
'We're all right Captain just bruised and grazed.'

Kirk and McCoy try to sort this mess out
Scotty opens the hatch and begins to shout
'Captain the Klingons are all around us'
While Spock logically said 'Don't fuss.'

The Phasers were issued to most of the crew
The one's who were fit and the injured too,
The battle commences, more casualties are had
To see such destruction was obviously bad.

Kirk's crew put up such a tremendous fight
There will be commendations by the end of this plight,
The starships repaired and the Klingons retreat
The Enterprise gives chase leaving Kirk on his feet.
With Deforest and Uhura sitting down on a rock,
'We'll be back soon,' was the message from Spock.

With Spock at the helm, the starship returned
Much wiser than most by the things he had learned,
'Beam us up Scottie' lets get back to work
Came the final order from Captain James T Kirk.

F Baker

Is it Saturday Today?

'Is it Saturday today?' asked the child of only three
   Many years ago. (And this is really true)
'Yes! So tidy up your toys and come and gobble up your tea.
   We musn't miss the time for Dr Who.
Remember that the Doc and Pete got trapped and can't get out
   But the dear old Doc is clever, they'll escape I have no doubt.'

In the evening light, the TV on, Mum settled in her place.
   The child, with tension mounting grew intent,
Spiralled with the music to a distant time and space.
   Through the tunnel to another world he went.
Wide of eye, mouth held open, concentration on his brow,
   Watched the Doctor think and plan, to get them out somehow.

'Look out!' he screamed 'The monster's here' It was a fearsome fight.
   (Switch off, his mother thought, but wouldn't dare.)
He puckered up his little face but kept the screen in sight,
   And backed away, to hide behind the chair.
From this safe haven, then, he saw the Doc and Peter win
   And run back to the Tardis. But! What's this? They can't get in.

'Diddle de dee. Diddle de dee,' the music sank away.
   He sighed and there were tears on his cheek.
'It's safe to come out now. You've got another hour of play'
   No answer, for he didn't want to speak.
A week was such a long, long time when you were only three,
So 'Is it Saturday today?' was then his daily plea.

Marjorie E Norton

The Star Ship

Captain's log star date, six seven five 'o' two
Another mission for Captain Kirk and his crew.
The star ship Enterprise is the place to be,
This flying fortress is a real sight to see.
Boldly going where no one has been before
Defying the greatest odds to enforce the law.
Going into action they will never know,
If they will stay alive, or their dreams will go.

Captain's log star date, six seven five 'o' three
Clingon's on the warpath, on the screen you see.
'What the hell do they want, tell me Mr Spock?'
'Apparently Captain, to give us a nasty shock.'
'I need more power lets go faster Mr Scott.'
'Aye, aye Captain, I will give you all she's got.'
'Now, tell me Mr Chekov are they catching us?'
'No chance Captain, not in that supped up bus.'
'Lieutenant Uhura can you hear their call?'
'No . . . no Captain there is no sound at all.'
'Is anyone hurt Bones, things were getting hot?'
'Everything is fine Jim we didn't take a shot.'

Captain's log star date, six seven five 'o' four
Clingon's left behind, will bother them no more.
Kirk will tell Starfleet, the crew were so brave
And that for him they would go to their grave.
Putting their lives at risk on each sordid trip
On Starfleet commands most famous ship.
When starships appear the villains all disperse
They'll keep star trekking around the universe.

K J Simpson

The Technician

They brought her in, weary, battered, and torn.
My orders and instructions, to make her ready by dawn.

Battle scarred she had done as asked.
But now needed help for the final task.

I have worked on some of the best.
This ship responds to all the tests.

She was eager to get the final job done.
Battle was no place for a lady, and not much fun.

I worked and laboured on her all night.
Every circuit had to be just right.

By daylight the job completed.
I hope she never gets defeated.

I had done my utmost best, she is now ready for her test.

I could wait three years or more.
No one knows the score for sure.

She is the lady of the skies, the solar systems her domain.
Keep her safe, till she needs my help again.

Precia Pitt

22

Aliens

A long time ago
In our ship we saw a glow,
We crash landed on sight
To a dismal planet with hardly any lights.
It was windy and cold
Plus a sense of being old
We entered the dome
Looked as if no one was home,
But all around us
Was a silence we hadn't judged
Armed with guns and big rockets
Plus ammunition full in our pockets.
Tapping came from beneath our feet
Should we go forward or retreat
Through this webbed like tunnel
There was noises through air vents and funnels
To our dismay
What we found on display,
Were big open topped eggs
With a creature above with long legs.
It came down beside our faces
We all fired at different places
The pods all exploded
And the creature was eroded,
But from how they were made
The thoughts we will take to our graves
If we have committed any sin
We just hope no more aliens will begin.

Linda Bailey

War of the Worlds

They say that Beeton's been invaded
by alien force they're all paraded
into the vat of radiation
the heart's torn out of our own nation.

This news I'm bound by truth report
to tell the world I must retort
will they touch me before I do
and change the news to what's untrue?

I've seen the signs of interference
and watched our citizens endurance
they're changed from inside so it's hidden
then they must do whate'er they're bidden.

It's not just only a few of our people
but a mass transference at the double
so do watch out there's louts about
and keep alert, oh please don't doubt.

If you escape the dreadful force
the truth for me you must endorse
for on the box some news reporters
have fallen foul of alien doctors.

A cover shrouds the very existence
of mother earth and all it's citizens
so keep an open mind pray do
and debate at length to find what's true.

Lorna May Noah

Hitchhiker's Guide to the Galaxy

Blake went on a journey
Well beyond his scope.
All the children knew that,
Not their parents: They'd no hope.

They seem to think that people
When out of sight will crack.
We have faith, in our hero
We know he will come back.

He's well equipped and knowledgeable.
Does anybody know
Where he'll be tomorrow
No matter where he goes?

That's Living that's what children think.
Why do adults, always shrink
Away from things, that are not real.
Fantasying doesn't kill.
Uncanny things, do cause a thrill.

Alien life we must explore
For they'll be there for ever more
How does their conversation go?
Do they have to work or no?

Is their intellect on hold?
Forward wind, or back or slow?

Are they progressing or regressing
In a different Galaxy?
Does time stand still at their command
Has destiny a leading hand?

Jill Ives

The Intrepid Dr Who

That well known Doctor of many a guise
Is extremely thoughtful, clever and wise
He saves the day from many a foe
And makes *time travel* safer, and so
What countless adventures he had with his friends
And many a *baddie* had to make amends
He righted wrong, as only he could
And was always on the side of good.
As soon as his *time machine* touched the ground
Aliens so dread, were all around
So with hardly a moment to gather his wit
He would wade into the fray, as spellbound we would sit,
Clued in awe, to our TV screen
Some less valiant of us, were heard to scream.
But dauntless our hero would win the day
Before the evil aliens could ever hold sway
And although he has changed in looks many a time
Honour and Trustworthiness from his face did shine,
And dazzle all who tried to fight him to win
At the end of the battle the victor would be him
And he would step into the *Tardis* and away he would go
On his next frightening mission to fight the foe.

Rosina Rust

A Trek to the Stars

Upon the Starship Enterprise
A voyage through the stars
High above earth's atmosphere
Speeding fast past Mars.

Legendary crew on board
Spock and Captain Kirk
Destroy the Klingons easily
Where ever they may lurk.

Action in every solar system
Excitement fills the air
As a new adventure starts
The Enterpise is there.

Flying above the speed of light
Action lies ahead,
No panic when danger arises
There's nowhere they fear to tread.

Beam me down Scottie
As the team descend once more
To boldly go to a new planet
Where no man has been before.

Kate Scales

The UFO

As I was driving from the mart
with cow and calf in tow,
I cast an upward glance and saw,
above, an UFO.

It hovered for a moment brief
and touched down close at hand;
I did not rush but calmly stopped
when I observed it land,

For wonders never cease, say I,
in such an age as this,
and my philosophy in life
is one of hit or miss.

And from this strange contraption's womb
emerged a queer sight -
a demon green with eyes like stars;
but I did not take fright.

We struck a bargain there and then;
it seemed an honest deal.
He bought with UFO'ish cash
the cow with calf at heel.

But I discovered at the bank
the currency was void.
With groans, the bankers shook their heads;
but I was not annoyed.

'Tis true I'd lost the cow and calf,
but something with me stays -
a precious memory unique,
to treasure all my days.

Dewi W Thomas

Stardrifter

He set intrepid eyes
on Alpha Centaurus
swung the Astro Launcher
into G minus X mode.
Flowed orbit-free
space lanes easily,
through mental patterns
painted neon-white.

Earth was unkind,
Space was a newer
vista, in the year
twenty five and four.
Sirius shone full bright
now. Planets vast
in veiled profusion
passed un-noticed.

At warp speed, days
and weeks slid
into years, light years
where spacemen age;
become lost in time.
Time has sapped
away his crew:
he was alone
seeking other worlds.

Ernest Ward

Doctor Who and the Tardis

The *Tardis* in the shape of a blue telephone booth,
Comes to a shuddering stop,
My name is Dr Who, I have just arrived from planet Pluto,
The *Tardis* or the telephone booth opens slowly,
I peep out warily, where have I landed?
On the screen it says planet X, the year O,
It could be anytime, anywhere in the future or in the past,
Craggy rocks and mist swirling, in another time and cold,
Something is moving, something is approaching, I quickly hide,
Cybermen! I have returned, I do not wish to come into contact
with them,
They search around, then silently they leave again,
I quickly escape into the *Tardis*
I shall return to planet Earth,
Through the skies of time, through the wonders of yesterdays,
Planets hurl by as I orbit the sky,
Colours of life exploding, shimmering, beaming beneath the
moons glow,
The sun leaping flames, frightening awesome in its beauty,
The planet earth nears, nearer, nearer,
I have landed again, I step from the safety of the *Tardis*,
The soft earth welcoming, green grass and blue seas,
Suddenly I feel cold and desperately afraid,
It is to quiet, there it is, approaching the metallic sound,
The sound of my enemy,
I am a Dalek . . .

M Bowers

Alien to Spocky

Can you work magic with your ears, Mr Spock?
Were you touched by a little green man?
Do they do something mystical, likely to shock?
If you flap them, can you fly over final frontiers?

I'm mystified by your appearance: it's weird.
Quite alien from my life on Planet Earth.
I'm bound to describe them as truly absurd.
What on earth must your mother have thought at your birth?

Perhaps you belong to some pixified cult:
An agency based yonks of light years away.
Where everyone else looks the same as yourself.
Where little Spock clones are born every day.

That's it! A clone planet - an engineered state:
An orbit where no one has gone before.
With a central controller manufacturing Spocks . . .
Transported to earth and sold in a store.

No wonder you're beaming, and it's all systems go.
You've seen off the Ninjas and fads through the years.
Foiled assassinations with your cosmic fo . . .
I'm sure it's because of the power in your ears.

So carry on trekking, you starship warrior.
Fight your good missions, don't let evil win.
Twitch your ears, Spocky, I'm coming to join you.
Beam me up Scottie, I'm on the next plane.

Audrey Fairclough

31

For Them All

Everyone needs to suspend disbelief
How else do children grow?
Everyone needs a fantasy land
Action grand
An heroic band,
How else can we create bricks out of sand?
How else make bread out of dough?

Everyone needs a family time
That half-hour in front of the box
Everyone needs to escape for a while
Exchanging a smile,
Steal the enemy's phial
Everyone needs to be part of the guile
Ignoring the ticking of clocks.

Jan Jones

Saturday Night Escape

Theme tune bristling up hairs on back
Children hiding behind sofa
Story continues from last week
Will Dr Who manage to escape?
Run Doctor Run,
Two minutes left
Sibermen about to extinguish all known life.

A bid to control the whole Galazy
The Doctor remembers an old trick,
Smartly reactivates a global revolutionary
Ridding the earth of the dreaded Sibermen
The Doctor and his Assistant decide it's time to leave.

Back to the tardis
It's time to press the button
Relief as the box safely disappears into space.
New adventure for time lord next week
Meanwhile children gingerly reappear.

Sue Barker

Conveyance

Once again we venture
Into the unknown
Through the universe
So vast
Enduring pleasure of
Extreme horror
Fearlessly we go
With the Star Trek cast.

Aboard the Starship
Enterprise
Transported who knows
Where,
What's our destination?
Who or what shall we
See out there?

Each voyage opens new
Horizons,
Galaxies, celestial bodies
Undiscovered,
With Captain Kirk and
Mr Spock,
The log book unreservedly
Recorded.

M Turner

Star Trek Fleet

Captain Kirk is calm and
bright when Klingon's
appear he'll put up a fight.

When Dr Spock says it's not
logical, we must believe him
as he's incredible.

Scottie knows what's best for
the ship, when danger lurks
he's the skip.

When the battle is over, the
enemy have gone, the
Starship Enterprise sigh,
it's over we've won.

So, the fleet travel off to a new
place, high in the sky, out into
space.

P Heath

Planet of the Apes

I am lost
now I am on a planet
forgot,
where are the people
I cannot see
as there is only me.
But I hear a noise
the noise grew louder
as I began to shake
I looked up
beyond belief
there stood
four apes
looking at me
where am I?
This is a planet
for apes
not the planet
for the human
race.

Tracy Salt

TV Time Travelling

I always did like Sci-fi
I grew up in that age,
When strange unearthly happenings
and space were all the rage.

I quite adored old *Star Trek*,
with Sulu, Kirk and Spock,
in fierce conflicts with Klingons,
helped by old bones, The Doc.

Lost in Space was special,
they were a funny lot,
floating through the universe,
with that odd voiced robot.

Then came *The Survivors*
They were like none before.
The tale of those remaining,
after a nuclear war.

Blake Seven was exciting
Jenna, Avon and Cally,
zooming in their space ship,
to good causes they'd rally.

I was sixteen when *Star Wars*
exploded onto the screen,
and fell in love with Hans Solo,
so macho, cool and mean.

Best of all the sci-fi films,
which terrified us kids,
was all about some lethal plants
in *Day of the Triffids*.

And now a generation on,
the march of time it cheats,
as with my kids, I settle down,
to watch sci-fi repeats!

Jacqueline D Price

Trekkies' Chant

Beaming down to a mysterious planet,
is the same old group of five,
Kirk, Spock, McCoy, plus two security guards,
who we know won't make it back alive.

They're responding to a distress call,
picked up by Uhura's intercom,
and soon they're outnumbered by aliens,
who Kirk will fight on a one to one.

And if there is a girl around,
be she blonde, green-skinned or purple-haired,
Kirk will always show her how to kiss,
though it's to the Enterprise he's really paired.

While phasers fire into energy clouds,
and dastardly Klingons enter *The Neutral Zone*,
Spock communes with the Ship's computer,
and in sickbay Kirk is checked over by Bones.

And every time Kirk needs more warp speed,
Scotty frowns and pulls a face,
'Aye Capt'n I'll canna' do my best,
but there's a chance we'll be stranded in space.'

Wherever the Enterprise might venture,
we all know for ever more,
that Kirk will always triumph,
Where no man has gone before.

Alyson Faye

Sonnet to Space

Hitchhike the galaxy of your mind
And let the Babel fish translate,
Leave conventional constraints behind
Explore some other ship of fate.
Take the cosmic road, and explore
All the worlds that life can hold.
Taste every cup, open every door,
The improbability drive is bold.
The past, the present, all conspire
To hold you in a spiral trap;
Look to the future to stir the fire,
Take a chance on the travellers' map:
Only you create stars anew,
Only you can find your 42.

Sara Bond

What was it

At the end of a lovely day
The sun was going down
My children had departed
And I was all alone.
It was then I could see it
Sitting there on a cloud
I just couldn't describe it
But I'm sure it was round.
On the edge of that dark cloud
I could see six red lights
As I sat there watching
They shined very bright.
I sat as in a trance
Time seemed to stand still
It wasn't until it disappeared
I felt weak and ill,
then I phoned my daughter
To tell her what I had seen
She laughed and said don't worry
It just couldn't have been.
All this time I've wondered
At what I really saw,
There is no way of knowing
There's no proof anymore.

Dorothy Cornwell

A Ship Full of Stars . . .

E ndless adventures on a five year mission
N ever before has there been such a vision,
T o boldly go where no man has gone before
E ver onwards into the stars do our intrepid crew soar.
R ed alert, yellow alert, bridge to transporter
P rimed for action, many a klingon vessel has fought her
R eady for anything, under Captain Kirk's command
I nto the universe and legend, hand in hand
S pock, *Bones*, Uhura, Sulu, Chekov, Scotty and Kirk
E veryone's final frontier, it's logical work.

Barnaby Jones

Remember

Do you remember the night
Lights flashed
And little green men danced
On the lawn
Beside the house
As we watched from the upstairs
Window?

And do you remember how we,
Holding our breath for fear of discovery
Tiptoed downstairs,
Through the back door,
Then on towards that large cylindrical
Shape
Which beckoned us
Then, vanished as we,
Shuddering,
Hid behind the apple tree
Too scarred to approach any further?

And do you remember how
On waking the next morning,
We assumed it all a dream
Until we stumbled upon
That small luminous green shoe
Abandoned among the daffodils?

Helen Peacocke

Beam Me Up Scotty

Star/Date: delayed,
Attention! Red Alert, the communications piped,
Automatically the crew were at their battle stations,
'Captain, a very large Klingon vessel is ready to fight,
a new battle cruiser it seems.' 'What's that vibration?'

'Sir, it's a sophisticated sort of tractor beam dilation,
even though our shields are up, it's trying to get hold,"
Thank you Mr Spock, keep posted, open communication,'
'Sir, we are out flanked.' 'Spock it's time to be bold.'

'Captain I'm only bringing this fact to your attention,'
'Sir, I have the Captain of the Klingon vessel for you,'
'Give me screen visual and computer translation.'
'Ah! James T Kirk, your death is well and truly overdue.

You are caught in our beam, soon it will tear you apart,
Kirk you have violated Klingon airspace and will die,
with your crew and the Enterprise, I have no heart,
and I will enjoy squashing you like a fly.'

'Screen off. Engineering, Scotty can we break free?'
'Aye Sir! dropping our shields, may give us the wedge,'
'I'll trust you with our lives, for Scotty, you are our escapee,
Thrusters on full now, we must have that edge.'

The star ship USS Enterprise managed to pull free,
and the Klingon battle ship was caught off guard,
and with Neutron torpedoes were blasted into space debris,
putting to an end for the time being, the Klingon's charade.

After some well earned shore leave on the planet Earth,
Mr Spock, Dr McCoy and Captain Kirk with camaraderie,
headed back to their only real home, a star ships berth,
with the immortal words uttered, *Beam me up Scotty.*

David Dawrant

Spock

It should wrap one about
like a soft cloak, answer
all dreams, desires and needs
be food and life and love
for mind and body, sponge away
the heat of animal demands, cool
control the weakness of poor flesh.
It is logical that logic should do this,
and therefore I desire
it will be so, and under its strait bands
I'll live my life all quietly till its end.

And yet -
    I must think, not feel
cast the net of my mind outward to my work,
            music, science -
                    all that logic serves,
            turn it away
                    from myself,
            deny that I am
                    animal
            alive, have breath and blood, can touch,
    deny my eyes can see
                    your smile
    deny
            my hand
                    its wish to reach
                            for yours.

Margaret Sillwood

45

Universal

Imagine you're there
Up amongst the stars,
Inside the celluloid
Showing tonight in your room.
The Utopia they show us is purely
Entertainment fantasy.
Or is it?
Race equality we fight for,
Klingons and Federation made it.
Answers from a machine,
Intelligent computers are here.
Knowledge beyond our realm,
We're always finding out.
Do the film makers truly
Give us a glimpse of what could be?
Childhood features enjoyed still
By adults, a search for reality,
A hope that somehow out there
Mankind has bettered himself.

Leena Edmunds

The Borg

It out thinks Picard and all his crew,
They're blocked at every turn.
It matches speed and orbit too,
Warf's lasers cannot burn.

The starships lines are smooth and sleek,
It orbits 'round the planet.
Its armoury is far from weak,
It hovers like a gannet.

What puzzles me is how Borg glides,
Can travel so fast up there.
Considering its awesome size
It's really just a square!

Square orbits? I'm no spaceman, sure;
But that defies all reason.
That ugly cube must not endure -
Borg shooting's now in season!

E Balmain

47

A Vulcan Dream

Captain Kirk this is Mister Spock, permission to speak,
May I convey some thoughts, which I hope you will not mock,
I had this vision of unseen eyes in unseen places,
Looking down on your Earth from unseen faces,
It would appear that millions or billions of miles away,
There are minds of the Universe that observe Earth's day,
What do they make of what they see,
Are Earthlings considered an oddity?

Such quaint customs can be seen,
Morris Dancing on the green,
Posting to each other minute boxes of wedding cake,
To be consumed at a gluttonous rate,
Miles and miles of traffic jams,
Fast food restaurants close at hand,
Dashing here, hurrying there,
Little love and patience anywhere,
Give us speed that's what we need,
You destroy your Planet at an alarming rate,
What would these minds make of such a state?

Would emotions fall to pieces,
Or could your Earth accept a superior species?
My logic tells me the answer has to be no,
The inhabitants of your Planet being totally illogical,
Rigid in thought and deed,
The main considerations would be their needs.

What do you make of my thoughts, Captain Kirk,
Of these things unseen,
Perhaps they are just peculiar to a Vulcan's dream?

Shirley Boyson

Memories of Doctor Who

All those years, yet memories clear
To the days when I was a lad
We would surround the TV
And watch Dr Who, my brothers,
Sisters, mum and dad.

Dr Who, the great time master,
Living in the future, living in the past,
His time machine, the Tardis, takes him there
The years passing by in a flash.

Where are my friends, where is the laughter?
Time took my mum and dad too,
The Tardis is the only answer,
I wish I was like Dr Who.

Now I'm old and gaze into space
With nothing left but tears
If only I could turn back time
Oh, how I miss those golden years.

Dr Who take me in your Tardis
To the best years I ever had.
I just want to watch you on TV
With my brothers, sisters, mum and dad.

Robert Conning

An Old Boiler

There was I alone, except for my dog
Watching TV on a Wednesday night
Tuned into Star Trek, 6.00 pm, BBC 1
Captain Kirk ordered *Beam them up Scotty*
When with a whoosh and a bang
My dog and I flew inside the TV set
No! We hadn't been beamed up and transported
The boiler in the cupboard had exploded
No more Kirk and Spock for me
Until I can afford to buy a new transmission set.

P Varma

Parallel

Worlds, side by side
Destined to collide.

Hally got his sums wrong
Comets showers do return
Their debris has not gone.

Side by side, worlds collide
It wasn't the atom bomb.

Children into adults grow, their
kindness, friendship, all must go.

God above sees it all
Humanity must fall.

Pool your honesty, share your grief
Humans deserve no better,
Children only know innocence
Adults can't live together.

C of E and Catholic, share blackboard
with Muslim and Hindu,
God above sees it all, but
What in heaven can he do.

Side with us, the cry comes up,
We are all *your* children
But I won't sit with him or her
Their customs are more than I can bear.

Help me God, the heathen's cry
Call me up when I die.

And make me good
And make me well
Safe from the jaws of hell.

But do not sit me near the others,
They have heathen fathers, and mothers
Only put me near my kind,
I won't mix with the others
Whose faith is different from my own,

Ezekiel saw four sides of your face,
When worlds collide and all must end
Do religions fervour bend
and each is given a place
Side by side.

Jean Elizabeth Bradley

Tommy Knockers

Where Einstein minds are twelve a dime,
  And they can all be read,
Exertion shows, paid through the nose
  For work that left them bled.
And eerie light shines 'neath the door,
  Sickly green, it oozes through,
Flowing, glowing, seemingly knowing,
  Beaming out to capture you.

Fetid air will choke you there
  Till time when all *become*;
And lungs will change, will rearrange
  As minds become as one.
Invert your mind. Seem weak, be strong.
  Think nought but false and tell true,
Or faded, jaded, you will have aided
  Tommy Knockers breaking through.

Cherry Tompsett

2001 - With Apologies to ACC and SK

Feel *Zarathustras* thundering might
Hearald a mystifying monolith
As forefather *Moonwatchers'* senses take flight
Homo Sapiens no wiser with magic and myth.

Inter-stellar submarine, *discovery*,
With sinister *Hal 9000* on board.
Of man the heavens make a mockery,
And will incessantly continue to goad.

Time is nigh for *Hal's* mutiny
And futuristic bedlam ensues
But Bowman's desperate for his destiny
Ensures this battle he shall not loose.

Cavernous emptiness eternally unfolding
To embrace with softly silken arms
Must we retreat to embryo unknowing
Of the angels and their silent psalms.

Tony Wilson

Once a Week Only

My flight of fancy takes me weekly.
On a journey through the skies.
Captain Kirk in charge of the bridge.
On the *Starship Enterprise*.
My seat reserved near a window.
Not far away, the lift door.
I wait, breath baited to boldly go,
Where no man has gone before.
Officer Uhura head turned, smiles hello,
Messrs Chekov and Sulu great I find.
Doctor McCoy waves a hand in greeting.
I am welcome. They're so very kind.
Science Officer Mr Spock.
Behaving with true Vulcan flare.
Mr Scott well respected. Not without reason.
He keeps *Enterprise* in the air.
SOS what awaits on an unexplored planet.
Some beings with hardly a thing on.
A Romulan tyrant caring only for power
Or an old adversary the Klingon?
Those designated investigate.
Unravelling problems that clog.
The villains are dealt with. Once more calm prevails
It's all there in Captain Kirk's log.
Back at warp speed, my fantasy over.
I know some folk think I am dotty.
But If I thought I could be Mr Spock's lady
I would yell out loud, 'Beam me up Scotty.'

Violette Edwards

A Trek into Space

Inner space, outer space, how can we earthlings know which one
                                                is which?
Sci Fi or Hi Fi, what a lot of difference and how does life go
                                                without a hitch?
There are weird sightings and movements and things that go
                                                bump in the night,
or is it just a friendly team of space travellers, like the Starship
                                                Enterprise in flight.

With Mr Spock from the planet Vulcan, not our Dr Spock from earth,
there is his helper Dr McCoy, known as Bones, always proving
                                                his worth.
Scotty the engineer, an invaluable man without who the Starship
                                                would fail.
He is there when all is lost to sort out the running, so all will be a
                                                plain sail.

There are many others who help things run well and keep the
                                                Starship alright.
Captain Kirk the protector, boss of them all keeps things running
                                                smoothly in flight.
He unlike Spock has human feelings and he cares for all of his staff.
Spock has no such emotions and understands that others do but
that does not get in his path

Star Trek followers are *Trekkies* they follow every adventure of
                                                Kirk and his friends.
Do they really believe I wonder, but it could be true, does it just
                                                the truth bend?
How do we really know what goes on in space, what lurks out
                                                there to be found?
So Scotty, my friend, if needed please beam me up, to keep
                                                me safe and sound.

Jil Bramhall

Whatever Happened to Princess Leia?

In my younger days I made a dreadful mistake,
An Ewok baby was the price I paid.
He was 3' 2" and incredibly cute,
I never guessed he could be such a brute.
I gave him my love, he wanted my body,
With chirruping sounds he took my virginity,
My friends told me, 'Don't trust that furball!'
But his fluffy face was my downfall.
He took my love and threw it away,
When I told him I was pregnant he left the same day.
What a way to leave a Princess, in a state of shock,
Never trust a man, even less an Ewok!

Ruth Burgess

Journey to Inner Mind and Space

Who is this I see before me?
An adult, an insult!
No wait, for I see beneath this leathered skin -
a child from long ago with twinkling eyes and infant grin.

Captain Kirk you travel to pioneer.
You bring your Vulcan, taking scientific stock,
big ears, by name of Spock,
with scrutinising eyes that seem at times to leer.

This planet is of children only!
For you and crew you'd live a life aged and lonely.
You see Never Never knows no bounds,
nor any need for any cure.
Reading your adult thoughts this astounds,
and you're not really sure.

But if you care to close your eyes,
and think of happy thoughts, fun and games, lots of play,
then open your eyes, you've Never Never really left your earth.

Into the mirror a child you see,
now all becomes fantasy,
which in turn becomes ecstasy.
Your mind is how you feel,
without playing down the real.

Innocent stories, nursery rhymes,
for the child within breaks through life's crimes,
and long live folklore -
to pioneer planets galore.

Paul Stocks

Conversation

And the Moon said to the Sun,
Hey, mister, why you always so hot?
With all that explodin' and flashin'
You hurt my eyes with all that damn light!
I can't get near you
For fear of goin' blind or gettin' burnt -
Why you like that, man?
And the Moon was sad and angry.
And the Sun said to the Moon,
What you complainin' about, Moon?
You got me to warm you when you were cold,
You got your world to sail around
All beautiful and mysterious and magic.
Moon, you got plenty.
You don't know how much plenty you got.
I am what I am,
And without what I am you got none of these things.
And the Moon thought,
I am what I am,
And Sun only ever warm half of me.
But too close would burn
And too far would freeze,
And I have my world
And Sun have no world,
And without me Sun have no-one to talk to,
And without Sun I have no warmth at all.
Sun is sun because he got no other thing to be,
And Moon is me.
And Moon said,
Sun, I don't reflect nothing
But what is mutual.

Maggie Thompson Hoskins

59

The Stars

Zap! With the lasers blue and white,
It's the bad guys we're all here to fight.
Destroy the Death Star and kill Darth Vader,
The Princess is captured so try and save her.

Our ten year mission is to explore,
But we always seem to find a war.
The end of the story is no surprise,
As we wave goodbye to the Enterprise.

Is it a bird or is it a plane?
It's Superman of course, or so they claim.
He flies through the air at the speed of light,
Putting all evil villains to flight.

Land of the Giants and Lost in Space,
Blake Seven is gone without a trace.
All Sci-Fi is good versus bad,
A hangover from a Sixties fad.

Dave Briggs

The Fifties

The fabulous fifties suspended in time.
A decade of delight and memories divine.
Cocooned in an oyster with pearls falling free.
Showing future generations how good life could be.

Marilyn Munroe star of the screen.
Elvis Presley, the enigmatic James Dean.
These were the people who had the common touch.
Influencing millions and contributing much.

Listening to The Goons on the radio.
Dashing to the theatre to catch a West End Show.
Guys and Dolls enlightened as *Paint Your Waggon* came.
My Fair Lady - *Kismet* - *The Pyjama Game.*

I was lucky to be there at the dawn of rock and roll.
Life was optimistic so few were on the dole.
Myriads of dancers with petticoats galore
Flocked to the Palais and rocked across the floor.

This was the era of the Coffee Bar
At the Two I's in Soho a youngster would go far.
With his guitar playing he soon was in the news.
No less than Tommy Steele it was singing the blues.

The television industry was growing day by day.
Love it or loathe it this media was here to stay.
We would be better now informed, television was *Cool*
A whole new generation brought up on Muffin the Mule.

I gave my heart in the fifties to a man who was not mine.
We loved and laughed a lot, a perfect precious time.
Will I be forgiven for what happened way back then.
The fifties and my lover will never come again.

Kate Jackson

Living in the Fifties

One thing stands out in the fifties
  Is that I left school,
And my father drove me homeward
  From the land of school and rule.
I then went into the business,
  Worked in the bookshop every day,
Loved every minute of it
  Selling books along my way.
Another thing I can remember
  Which is very close to me,
King George died and Elizabeth
  Was crowned Queen for all to see.
We all crowded in our lounge,
  Watched it all on our TV
Saw our wonderful Queen crowned
  It was marvellous to see.
Another thing in the fifties
  Which helped me in my life,
Billy Graham held his crusade
  And it did away with strife.
I became a Christian convert
  And God helped me year by year
To live a better life
  And do away with fear.
Yes living in the fifties
  Was a very great decade,
It helped me to see
  The future way my life was made.

Jean M Webster

A Child's View of Liverpool - December 1952

Rattling down town
on a tram car,
Saturday, with Mum and Dad,
Stalls at the back of the market,
Selling puppies
looking cold, and so sad.

Then Church Street
and the wonder of Woolworth's,
A treasure trove untold,
Toys in the weeks before
Christmas, a
fairy tale world to behold.

Now a trip to the Grotto
to see Santa, and
Cinders this year at her ball,
Colour, enchantment and beauty,
Childhood memories that
never will pall.

Carole H Sexton

1953 - Coronation Year

In the year of the Coronation
We all had a wonderful celebration,
People had parties all of the day
Even Mount Everest was climbed in May.
Queen Elizabeth was crowned in June
And everybody danced to a joyous tune.
Bands throughout the land were playing
People in Westminster Abbey were praying.
Flags and banners were gaily flying
And some children were noisily crying
Fireworks exploded in the sky
While rockets whizzed way up high.
In the year of the Coronation
We all had a wonderful celebration.

Ann Sylvia Franks

Short of Brass

When I were a little lass
Times were hard and short of brass,
None of the things we have today
Improvising in every way.
One up one down and scullery
Was how we used to live
No bathroom just an old tin bath
No loo inside but 'round the block.
Gas mantles on the fireplace wall
Wireless to entertain us all
We didn't have a lot of toys,
Yet still them days were good.
Parents were much stricter then
Children daren't argue with them
Don't argue, don't be rude,
Do as your told, be seen and not heard.
It didn't do us any harm
Made us able to conform
Gave us values never forgotten
In that age of weaving cotton.
Lowly folk, good and kind
Hearts of gold
The neighbourly kind.

Margaret A Threlfall

Korean POW

Dad never spoke about the war
He never spoke of dead men,
Though
He named us all after them.

Dad mentioned in passing
'The chinks were nae bad,
But if you didna' like
Fish and rice every day,
The food
Was nae gaed.'

Cameron Montrose

The Fifties

I count not the sorrows or the tears
As I recall the many passing years,
But take stock of the blessings and the glees
For young, and full of future was I in the fifties.
New names and rising stars like Hawthorn and Moss
When so much seem to lie ahead
And all was gain, and nothing loss
'You have never had it so good,' was the statement of the day.

The Welfare State and all good things were under way
New Knights in armour, old dragons would slay
And paradise would reign on full pay
The atom was for the future and definitely split
But united were the people, determined and full of grit
H E Bates created The Larkins and there was a lot of fun
But where has it gone - what have we done?

Clive Cornwall

A Fifties Childhood

I was a child of the Fifties
Born after the war torn years,
Unscathed by memories of Blackout and Blitz,
No nightmares of terror and tears,
Too young to fret about rationing,
But in awe of our first TV screen,
When neighbours crowded into our front room,
To view the Coronation of Elizabeth the Queen,
(And I still have a tattered Presentation Book,
With a treasured mug and spoon!)
Each week enthralled I watched Bill and Ben,
Andy Pandy and the Flower Pot Men,
And I recall the shock when I returned from school,
To hear there was to be no more Muffin the Mule.

With friends I romped freely in a nearby park,
Catching tiddlers and shrimps in a net,
Skipping home tired to confess to mum,
That my skirt and my knickers were muddy and wet.
Then a bath was taken in front of the fire,
In the tin tub dad brought in from the shed,
And we sang along with the Ovaltineys,
Before I was tucked up in bed.

I was a child of the Fifities,
Those days when the sun always shone,
Now I pity the child of the Nineties,
Don't talk to strangers. Violence. Dangers.
Days of freedom have gone.

Christine Pearce

The Ruby Jubilee

Forty years on since that great day
Of the crowning of our Queen
A beautiful sight that glorious day
That the world has ever seen.

She accepted that crown and all it meant
As she gave away her youth
A wife and a mother she already was
For her loyalty there was the truth.

She has travelled the world from end to end
Worn ermine jewels and such
But freedom was never her luxury
That we commoners value so much.

Her family grew up as all must do
And the branched spread on her tree
But then in one year all her happiness
Must have ebbed like the tide of the sea.

But why should they blame our Queen so proud
That has graced us for forty long years
For she is no different from you or me
With a heart that can break and bring tears.

Those forty years have been and gone
With no flags or pageantry fine
No fireworks, no bonfires, no buntings
And no street parties this time.

But she's that same Queen with a golden crown
That remembers the waving and cheers
But has suffered through time like the rest of us
May she reign for many long years.

C Hall

Memories are Made of This

I was fourteen and happily new nothing of the world.
With Laura began a journey which my young mind would unfurl.
Such anticipation! We travelled oh! So happy in heart,
From Leeds to Liverpool at speed, so eager to make a start.
Granny Scott was awaiting as we hurried up the wobbly gangway,
To us it was an ocean liner which had taken us far away!
Us, two young Leeds lasses were to stay with Laura's Granny Scott,
For our holiday in Belfast, it's raining, so what!
The little house up the *Shankill Road* buzzed with love and care,
We ate soda farls and champ, fresh dulse still smelled of the sea air!
Watching the orange marches not understanding motive or pride,
We walked alongside the big bass drum, and didn't want to hide,
Then to a cottage by the sea, Uncle Billy's Farm so rural,
Where Sally the big old Irish sow gave birth to piglets, plural!
The city and its monuments, the parks, the sea, the people,
Majestic wrought iron gates, some glorious church steeple,
Its wind blown flag always flying sadly at half mast,
The friends I made and so much loved, these I often miss,
In a wonderful place across the sea, a place we call Belfast.
I'm glad to hold those precious moments deep within my heart,
I, the young English girl cried when we had to part,
To granny I waved a loving hand, then I blew her a kiss,
So happy to have been and seen Belfast, seen in a child's eye,
For wonderful memories are made of this, and memories never die.

Joyce M Hefti-Whitney

70

Our Gracious Queen for Forty Years

We remember you when you were a little girl
I can picture you now, with those lovely curls
Then we watched you grow up, and in World War 2
You did a good task, a job to help us through
Then romance came along, and you made a beautiful bride,
As you walked down the Aisle, with Prince Philip by your side
But later the sad news came, when you lost your dad,
Then you became our Queen, the most gracious Queen we
                                                    have had.

Now you celebrate forty long years, reigning over us,
Always so loyal and true, never making a fuss,
You have had your ups and downs, through all those years,
Some were happy years, and a few brought some tears
May God give you his blessing, to be our Queen forever more,
Because we think the world of you, a Queen we all adore.

Olive Peck

Days of Past

Remember the days when the past jumped in front of you
Blocking your way,
Did you see your mistakes dressed in
a theatre of confusion?
How easy to forget after all what you recall is your work
Does love hold you up?
You showcase your extremes of nature
to hide your insecurities.
You parade your outspoken mind
Like some lethal weapon
Your humour is your protector
a fortress built on fear,
Your emotions have no identity
Your intentions are all too clear.
Can't you see there's someone who cares?
Who loves - with the spirit of understanding
Everyone has second sight in times of suffering
Like claw marks on the smooth plains of brilliance
A cry for help the picture is commanding
You're conversing with silence
And everybody hears.

Michael Strachan

The Fifties

Those were the winter years; high up
in the Old Kilpatrick hills we saw
the world from far off, through the steam
of boilers and the vats that hissed
and bubbled as the swill became
a sea of porridge to be poured
into the troughs, pail by scalding pail,
while the pigs screamed behind locked gates.

Work was day-long, wet and cold,
nights saw the weakly piglets, pink
and curled beside the Aga; we dropped
milk gently down protesting throats.

Then television came; the Queen,
greenish, far-off and crackly, swept
through the kitchen . . . and the bells,
the cheers, the waving flags and crowds
of the Coronation were there, were ours.

Life opened up - the world was ours:
a Morris Minor for two hundred pounds,
a three-piece suite for twenty, a new
TV. We chilled to Quatermass,
laughed with Bob Hope, but best of all

immediate news was ours; at night
driving the younglings from the field
down to the deserted yard,
we saw the arched sky differently.
We pictured Everest now scaled,
and Russia's Sputnik that was soon
to pierce the veils of space and dark
and give the world that first step on the moon.

Dorothy Whamond

Then and Now

The high weather-cock on the steeple top
has stuck where the wind sets fair;
a light sea-breeze stirs the sycamore trees;
and it's always summer there.

Bright sunshine falls on the old grey walls
of the church that sits on the hill;
and within the scope of the grassy slope
stand hundreds of headstones still.

The churchyard drops into the copse
over a twelve-foot wall,
where the speckled trout dart in and out
through the pool by the waterfall.

The weather-cock on the steep top
has rusted and fallen awry;
the rain pelts down on the squalid town
from a grim and lowering sky.

The church clock chimes at unusual times,
and three clock-faces are blank:
the fourth one sticks at half past six
with gravity to thank.

Bare, dripping trees lean ill at ease
over the turbulent stream,
strewn, alas, with broken glass
and littered with polythene.

Jim Mollison

As Time Passes

Did time stand still
when we walked along,
The lanes so green
And the birds in song.

Did you remember
That day in June,
When the fields with
Yellow were festooned.

You wished with me
That all would stay,
As peaceful as they
Were that day.

But life moves on
And so did we,
The fields are gone
There are no trees.

The concrete road
That spans the lanes,
We'll never find
That peace again.

Beryl Smyter

The Hollow Lamp

The awesomely nostalgic smell
Of the nocturnal cold
Reminds the most vulnerable and honest
Memory,
Of very safe cold nights
In childhood.

When the universe
Was a small, potentially cosy, yellow-lit
Room with a green baize table,
Simple chairs,
And a very thick chill
Blackness outside, reflecting

The room in the odd and lovely
Velveteen curtained window.
Now that room is at the bottom
Of the smallest part of our fragile heads.
Now the night lurches in
Re-defining the universe
As the true process of the planet:
First madness;
Then, physical destruction.

The unbeatable formula of evil.
Childhood's rooms must be the afterlife.

Jock Mills

Living in the Fifties

Living in the fifties
Well, I was still quite young
For I was still at Secondary Mod
My life had just begun.

But I remember clearly
The start of Rock 'n' Roll
With Teddy boys and Teddy girls
Holding hands as they did the stroll.

Bill Haley and his Comets
Little Richard doing his thing
While Mum and Dad with their Gramphone
Just wanted to listen to Bing.

My heart throb Elvis Presley
He really made me swoon
I remember while in cookery class
How I'd sing into the spoon.

My class mates used to love it
'Oh please Val, sing some more.'
So then I'd be the Platters
Then we'd dance around the floor.

The leaving dance dressed to the nines
We really looked the part
When we danced to Dickie Valentine
It nearly broke my heart.

I've many happy memories
But none of them so clear
As the start of good old Rock 'n' Roll
In my adolescent years.

V A Skelton

London Typist

1950's in an office,
That is, forty years ago.
Eighteen pounds the first month's salary,
Fare was very little though.
While you were the Library doggie,
Beat the machine in the typing pool.
Carbon paper, lots of rubbing,
All to *American Patrol.*

Yes sir, no sir, teleprinter,
Pitman's shorthand, answer bell,
Duplication by Gestetner,
Sellotape was new as well.

Package tours with Gin at sixpence,
Communism in the Park,
Lyons Corner House provided
Meals and Nippies after work.

Nat King Cole and Frank Sinatra
Kiss Me Kate, Pyjama Game,
Carousel and Oklahoma,
All before the NT came
Young Cliff Richard, coffee houses,
Beaverbrook and Picture Post,
Coronation, pre-sensation,
First Ascent of Everest.

They were Salad Days, the Fifties,
Sandy Wilson, *The Boy Friend,*
What a pity, and I mean it,
Such a good time had to end.

Jo Appleyard

The Storm

It was a dire beginning to '53
The Great Invasion of the sea
The swift unbelievable flow
That made the peoples' blood run slow
Struck with fear they could not cry
As loved ones out of reach swept by.

Lord give us strength and faith to pray
That we will live to see another day
Then in the distance could be seen
A man whose courage was supreme
He heaved the boat with all his might
And many lives he saved that night.

Not once but thrice he battled through
This young American brave and true
Then invited to the Palace at the Queen's request
He must have been pleased to be her quest
Little did he think that he would be
A quest in England in 1993.

H Whittmee

The Saturday Dance

Pencil skirt, long earrings
a must the rope of pearls
make-up on all ready
meet up with the girls.

Showing off while dancing
twist and rock and roll
friends all eyeing up the lads
each one has her goal.

Fancied him a long time
dark good looking Ken
just know he's going to ask me
burning question when?

Could it be the last waltz?
nervous to the end
is he coming straight to me?
Oh no! It's my best friend.

Joyce Battey

'Twas the Time

During the nineteen fifties,
'Twas the time when I was a boy,
When turban headed women
Chatted with so much joy!
We never had a telly
Or the luxuries you see today!
Or toys that cost so much to buy,
For us to go and play,
But we were just as happy
With hopscotch, top and whip!
And not forgetting home made toffee
That often burnt your lip,

For in the nineteen fifties
Coupons still applied
You couldn't buy what you wanted
Even if you tried!
Perhaps that's why I'm contented
With the simple things in life,
Like loving, living, and children,
And the heart of my dear wife.

Michael David Sparkes

Fifty Fifty

While reviewing my past
In the years of the fifties
Ventures tried - but none surpassed,
Instant luck I did not find
Security was me piece of mind.

Luck was a gift which eluded me
Never won a raffle or lottery,
Neither excelled in drive or pace,
Only saw myself in second place.

I settled for luck in a different way
Contentment - joy - from day to day.
Fast riches ceased to be my aim;
Content to adapt - whatever came.
This I accepted as wealth in kind
Yet one prominence, did spring to mind

In health my life had been enriched
Tho I'd never considered this as a gift.
Had the hand of fortune favoured me?
Was health the prize I did not see
And the stars once chased - imaginary.

'Was this my wealth' - disguised as health
That the Lord had bestowed on me.
Then if luck be health with piece of mind
I have left my friends; far, far, behind.

R L Bennett

Child's Time

Frogspawn hunters all set for fun,
red cheeks glowing in the midday sun.
Short pants torn, bloodied knees,
cowboys and Indians, then up shaking trees.

Open fields with dotted flowers,
yellow and white in buttercup mind,
blue skies and singing lark,
no money could find.

Distant noises of farmyard beasts,
not realising they'd all make feasts.
Quaint country smells pull back the years,
when small boy adventures played soldiers there.

Family favourites and roast beef days,
butterfly chases down sunny ways.
New mown grass for tickly battles,
shaking of the winter shackles.

Memories of times when violence was only,
the Saturday morning show where the
bloodstains were phoney.
Jumping the steams of bygone times,
when stolen gobstoppers seemed the worst of crimes.

David Buck

Electric Blue

I worked in Woolies in '55,
And sported a split way up the side
Of a straight skirt too narrow to walk.
Real money for records and groovy talk.
Flat bebop shoes at three and four,
We couldn't wait to get out the door
Beehives stiff and pony tails fly,
Sugar stiff petticoats swirling high
We'd dance all night to the rocking sound.
The brightest butterflies for miles around.
Our partners equal in bright electric blue,
Drain pipes, lace ties, long drapes too.
It was good, it was fun to be young and alive
And a rocking and a rolling in '55.

Collette Braillard Metcalfe

The Rag and Bone Man

Slowly, bumping over antiquated cobbles
     Wheels squeaking in discordant song
He used to come. Frayed jacked dull in grime,
     Trousers overlong, wrinkled trappings
Doubled into ancient boots.
     Raucous calls, stinging the morning air
'Rag Bone!' Rag Bone!'
     Forgotten paint flaking spokes,
A choir of dangling pans.

From his sweating horse steam rose,
     Nostrils pushed wide
Dark holes sucking gutter smells,
     Tembling withers, eager with anticipation
She'd nussle in my hand hunting sugar.
     Plodding frowning streets
Worthy workmate, generous
     In her service, jingling,
A patient slave in harness.

Gasometers, gigantic drums
     Reeking rotten-eggs and waste
Shadowed their steady path, under scowling slates
     The cart would wind its way,
Reflection stirring broken-glass and puddles.
     Torn petticoats with Grandma's corsets,
Bundled cast-offs cluttered
     Into chaos, yesteryear's pride
Become tomorrow's rags.

Now silent is the creaking wheel,
His voice a distant echo of a faded time,
A vague impression, sketched in pencil on my mind.

Jackie Huck

Kiss Curls

Oh, I remember the Fifties!
I was only a lass in my teens.
The Palais de Dance and Locarno,
And the Friday night Youth Club scene.

All jiving away to Bill Haley
and rocking all over the place.
Lonnie Donegan, Tommy Steele, Elvis
And Cliff with his *baby face*.

Umpteen net petticoats under our skirts,
All swirling about on the floor.
Stiletto heels with pointed toes,
Pin perms and kiss curls galore!

'Cos you couldn't sit down in those *undies*,
The net was all prickly and rough.
Those stilettos we loved were painful
But we still wore the silly stuff!

I remember walking home after the dances
My heels getting stuck 'tween the slabs.
Starched net petticoats over my arm,
And my shoes ending up in my bag!

Nottingham had its fair share of the *The Teds* -
Their suits made the older folk stare.
Drainpipe trousers in reds and blues,
And fluorescent-green socks everywhere!

And *those baskets* us girls carried around,
All wicker, and *heavy as lead*.
Snagging our nylons, an' jumpers, an' skirts -
We must have been *daft in the head!*

Val Hall

Elizabethans

We married in Nineteen Fifty,
Our wedding went very well,
The bridal clothes were borrowed
But no one else could tell.

Food was still on ration,
Clothes in short supply,
Furniture was *utility*,
It was all that you could buy.

When we expected a baby
Food coupons were still in use
But I got my extra rations
And bottles of orange juice.

We bought our very first telly,
Nine inches across, black and white
And we saw the Queen's Coronation,
We marvelled at the sight.

We now were Elizabethans,
Great Britain, proud to be
And Hilary scaled Mount Everest
Making such history.

There were lots of things we didn't have,
Some not yet invented
But we were alive in the fifties,
We were happy and contented.

Is it really forty years ago?
My word, how time has flown -
I'm on a Widow's Pension
And Elizabeth's still on the throne!

Patricia Catling

Micklefield in the 1950's

Cloth caps and clogs
Home pricked rugs
Streets with barking dogs
Blue and white striped jugs.

Drippin' in a jar
Cast iron frying pan
No-one has a car
Except the tally man.

Bath time Saturday night
Time for a good scrub
Standing there upright
In the peggy tub.

Father goes for a drink
Swears it does him good
Mother has to think
Can't see how it could.

Sunday morning breakfast
Now and then it's kippers
Working week is past
Time for pipe and slippers.

Monday morning wash day
Kitchen full of steam
All work no play
Comfort is a dream.

Dennis Best

I Remember Bubble Cars

A fifties child with braided hair,
gym tunic, lace up shoes
I wanted strappy patent ones
but they wouldn't let me choose!
I race across the linoleum,
cold beneath my feet and
I hurry and eat my grapenuts
to get my Saturday treat.
Wash my face with Wrights Coal Tar Soap,
brush my teeth with Pepsodent
and already in my mind's eye
I've got my sixpence spent!
First I'll buy some coloured chalks
or maybe a sheet of scraps
and then a lucky potato and
get my threepence, back perhaps.
With my pals I'll collect car numbers,
swop scraps, play double-dare
but we must never go near the river,
mum says *Polio hides there.*
There's a lion on my boiled egg
then Sunday School at the Mission,
I Love Lucy's on tonight -
yes, we have a television!
Nightie warmed on the fireguard,
this week's Bunty read -
See you later alligator
it's time to go to bed.

Thelma Boath

Young and Free

Oh! To be young and free,
Once again in the swinging fifties,
When dating was fun,
But sex! Never done!
Just something that one day could be,
A kiss and a cuddle,
That left your emotions in a muddle,
Longing to go further,
But scared you'd end up in trouble,
In the days when you never heard of *aids*.
Not knowing what the future would be,
We laughed, we sometimes cried,
Over handsome movie stars, we sighted,
Oh! To be young and free,
Back again in those swinging fifties.

Dorothy Langdon

Been Good to Know You

Let us stroll again through the Fifties,
With my memories most good, few bad.
The men folk grafters, their womenfolk thrifty,
And many the good time we had.

Our lives still bore those wartime scars,
From restrictions of food and sweets.
The children longed for the chocolate bars,
They received as a *ration day* treat.

For some, life's lottery once more brought grief,
By happenings, again fashioned by war.
Korea and Suez belied the belief,
That such sorrow would happen no more.

Everest conquered, a Queen installed;
The arrival of Teds, Mods, and Rockers.
Young ones delighted, elders appalled,
By the exposure of Marilyn Monroe shockers.

Television began to take over our lives,
By those alluring silver screens.
Persuasive adverts brainwashed our wives
Into believing that there is cleaner than clean.

Discipline reigned in our homes and schools,
Friendly bobbies were seen on the beat.
But, now in the Nineties anarchy off-time rules,
With law and order obliged to retreat.

Jock McGregor

The New Era

Living in the '50's was exciting to be sure,
With fashions changing every day,
And teddy boys galore,
How we used to hobble,
In pencil skirts so very tight,
Together with wedged high heeled shoes,
We must have looked a sight,
Wearing Garish lipstick,
We thought we were the tops,
And thick pan-stick makeup,
Which helped to hide the spots,
In February 1952, our beloved King,
Quietly passed away,
The country went into deep mourning,
As in ceremonial state he lay,
On the 2nd June 1953,
Came the coronation of Elizabeth 2nd,
Our very own young Queen,
The ceremony of the crowning,
Was the most solemn ever seen,
For those who had television,
It proved a busy time,
With friends and neighbours popping in,
And toasting her with wine,
As the '50's came to its close,
We gave a fond farewell,
And looked forward to the future,
With a new Queen at the helm.

Patricia Short

Living in the Fifties

I was a happy teenager,
In the Fifties, we had fun,
The *Flower Power*, Peace Man,
An era had begun,
Paper nylon petticoats,
Bobby socks and bows,
Hair all done in kiss curls,
All the latest clothes,
Bell bottoms and platform shoes,
Teddy boys with suedes,
Drainpipe trousers are in style,
Long hair for the *Neds*,
Living in the *Fifties*,
Was lots of fun for me,
Baubles, bangles, lots of beads,
Rock n Roll, set free,
Changes happen every day,
Though many years have gone,
Living in the *Fifties*, then,
I felt I did belong.

Janette Campbell

A Way of Life

I'll never forget
 when but a lad
  I went down the pit
   to work with me dad.
    And the weren't just me
     there were others too;
      sons of their fathers
       just out of school.

Yet a mile underground
 soon ended my dream,
  bent over double
   in a three foot seam;
    choking on dust
     wringing with sweat,
      in the light of a lamp;
       a moth wouldn't see.
        Digging the coal this country it saved
         and to be miners. Men of us made.

And I remember when I was eighteen
 and into the army I volunteered;
  not for the country I might add
   for I knew that if I left the pit;
    I'd be called up anyway.
     And the weren't just me
      the wer' others too,
       giving up a tradition;
        that we'd all outgrew.

K Casewell

A Fifties Teenager

The Fifties conjure up for me
Memories that used to be,
Billowing skirts and high heeled shoes
So many pretty things to choose.

I bought a car
And learnt to drive,
And with good music
Learnt to jive.

Rock and Roll was just the thing
That made me want to dance and sing.
Bill Haley played Rock around the Clock
It gave our parents quite a shock.

Dickie Valentine was so romantic,
And when Johnnie Ray cried he drove me frantic,
Outside theatres we would go
Queuing up for every show.

Now I'm a grandma I can see
What the fifties held for me,
Lots of fun for everyone
And especially for me.

Avril Wright

The Mermaid of Bridlington

She has no comb and glass in her hand
Nor tresses of golden hair
The cold North Sea's her hunting land
But sailors do not despair.

Her hair is dark with seaweed strands
And brown green are her eyes
The shimmering scales of her fishy tail
Sparkle in the night.

She opens her arms to the ships at sea
And bids them on their way
But curious sailors steer to view
Despite what legends say.

She slithers down rocks to play with fish
And sing to the seashells
When mists come down and storms ensue
She calls, 'Make haste away.'

And so if you sail on the Bridlington Queen
Or Yorkshire Bell this year
If you espy this Yorkshire lass
There is no need to fear.

Marian O'Sullivan

Those Were the Days

Expresso Bars
and coffee shops
coloured stockings
Saturday hops.
Teddy Boys
I thought looked cute,

Six-Five Special
boover boots.
White sports coat
bootlace ties
all the fashion
how time flies.
Beehive styles
winkle pickers
yards of net
which snagged
your knickers.
How we rocked
around the clock
in the best of
party frocks.
Happy halcyon
teenage years
when life was fun
and held no fears.

Now I know I'm not so nifty
For it's me that's in the Fifties!

Hilary Malone

Full Time Work and Carefree Leisure

The '50's - they were cracking good years -
        Goodbye '40's, the worries and cares.

Shortages yes, but very much hope -
        We'd had it tough, we could all cope.

Young *married's* shared homes with their in-laws -
        And saved up the *Divi* at the Stores.

There were jobs a plenty, no dole fear -
        To buy a house, everyone's idea.

Food was still rationed early in '50,
        But we survived 'cos we were thrifty.

Schools were full with the baby boom -
        And introduced the mobile classroom.

Babes were born at home, the midwife came -
        But the single mum suffered great shame.

The New Look was worn with great panache,
        Men - out of uniform - cut a dash.

Premium bonds were sold for the first time,
        CND Protesters jailed for crime.

We enjoyed The Bridge on the River Kwai,
        The African Queen, the King and I.

King George the 6th died, *Long Live the Queen* -
        The Coronation - a classic scene.

Hilary and Hunt scaled Mount Everest -
        Bannister's four minute mile was the best.

In the '50's people were honest and true -
Attitudes were kindly and caring too.

A decade to recall with pleasure -
Of full-time work and carefree leisure.

Pat Berkshire

Gone With the Wind-Up Gramophone

Days spent playing in the street
The car, a thing we'd rarely meet
The milkman's horse with tail that twitched
Would sometimes cross our *cricket pitch.*

Those summer days as I recall
It hardly ever rained at all
The sun shone done from skies of blue
Well, maybe that's not strictly true.

From minors then to almost majors
We became the first teenagers
We thought we were so sharp and bright
With ponytails and waists nipped tight.

Petticoats with tiers of netting
Sitting in the back row petting
Teetering on stiletto heels
In coffee bars of stainless steel.

Teddy boys with velvet collars
Thought they looked a million dollars
Drainpipe trousers were the news
DA's and beetle crusher shoes.

Rock and roll was just beginning
Adults thought we all were sinning
But when we had kids of our own
It was our turn to nag and moan.

It's true each older generation
Abhors the lack of veneration
From the young, who look like freaks
But like us, they'll soon be antiques.

Frances Cregan

The Coronation

I saw her there - a figure of delight
A picture that charmed my sight
Those blue eyes with joy were gleaming
Her bright smile with happiness beaming.

It was a very emotional scene
As the crowd chanted, 'We want the Queen.'
For many many hours they waited
When suddenly the noise abated.

On the balcony stepped the new young Queen
Beautiful - proud and serene
With a smile she waved graciously
Bringing from the crowd a cheer of ecstasy.

Then came the Royal Family
A truly glittering sight
Believe me 'twas no fantasy
I know - I was there that night.

Elsie Mary Hickleton

School in the Fifties

I recall the day I started school
My joy was mixed with fears
For what I thought was for a day
Lasted ten long years.

I remember my first teacher
The Headmaster was her man
With spectacles and a wee moustache
But the master hadn't one.

And so the lessons did begin
Which was a funny thing
My first task as a school boy
Was threading beads on string.

Then there was the music class
On wireless not TV,
Not many folk had one of those
In nineteen fifty three.

Then there was our Gala Day
With our brand new summer gear
Our streamers and our little flags
We were happy then all year.

But that was in the Fifties
It's all back in the past
And if I could go back again
I'd probably still come last.

Jock Butler

The 'We Must Have' Age

We must have a new house built my dear,
    Please get the building-permit today.
We must have a telephone too my dear
    Put our name on the list straight away.
We must have that latest vacuum cleaner
    The new carpets will need it for sure.
We must have those tinkling wind chimes
    We will place them by the front door.
We must have that clever washing machine
    That whisks all the water away.
We must have those gorgeous American-drapes
    Which were featured in *Home Fashions* today.
We must have a corner-bar my dear,
    Like the moneyed people do.
We must have a far bigger tele',
    Then our friends can come into view.
We must have a smart large caravan,
    An asset it will be for sure.
We must have a car to pull it along,
    Or else our lives will be such a bore.

Joyce Calvert

Proclamation - 1952

Our well loved King has passed in death -
God save the Queen Elizabeth.
Now sounds the trumpet's brazen notes,
Her standard in the breeze lone floats,
The cry goes up from myriad throats,
'God save the Queen, Elizabeth.'
Called when still young to dedicate
Her life in service to the State -
Her destiny, her noble fate -
God save the Queen Elizabeth.
The herald's trumpet now is blown,
The princess must go forth to own
The lonely greatness of the Throne -
God save the Queen Elizabeth.
Our well loved King has passed in death -
God save the Queen Elizabeth.

Milly Blane

Jive on

In the fifties chuck berry brought music alive,
Giving us the jitterbug and the Jive,
The fashions to go with it were so fine,
With socks and flared skirts so divine,
And the suits with jackets so long,
The style could live on and on,
To watch the partners jive around,
To the tremendous beating sound,
Really made you feel alive,
So long live jitterbug and jive.

L P Smith-Warren

World After War

With suffering of a world
War fresh in the memory
We are the lucky ones
Who lived into posterity.
Complete was the madness of all those years
Resources and energies were spent
Setting up a decade into lent
Accustomed to victory but over what?
The countries which still stood
Had their life sucked out by the after rot
America looked on in a pitiful vain
Whilst a new Europe began its rebuild
Bricks divided people trying to pick up the remains.
Younger generations eager to hatch promiscuity
Tried to follow parents proper path
Order and tradition held its last tenuous grip
As the teens prepared for their first rebellious sip.
At a time in history when values became misunderstood
The young rocked and the good times rolled
Racing into a future of new fads, that fashion sold
Gone were the days of stagnance.
Everyone looked for modern bends and new found trends
Setting society up on a fast lane expense
Living day to day forgetting recompense,
A world had enough of suffering.
Its people were now ready for a state of mind that lead
To technology and a mcarthuristic hatred of red
A decade that in history was to be the most transformed
From the aftermath of turmoil
To a self satisfaction that became inbred

(Thank you to Alexa for all your help)

David Goldblatt

106

Living in the Fifties

Ration books had burned in Trafalgar Square
Then were happy mothers beneath Lord Nelson's stare,
As coupons were no longer needed to buy a piece of meat,
Why did those crafty butchers raise prices and thus cheat
The poor and needy, who had almost forgotten how
To cook and enjoy a Sunday roast, whether a piece of old bull or
even an old cow?
But Suez proved a blessing in one special way
For we learner drivers could drive alone all day!
That suited me a learner, very late in life.
Just able to afford a car and support a wife!
A move was in the offing and fate had decreed
We should uproot ourselves and on new pastures feed!
When opportunity knocked, the chance could not be ignored,
But the problems created hurt the family I adored!
There followed months of heartache and tension,
With family bereavement deserving a mention!
What a scramble life became for almost a year,
Until in the end the road ahead had become quite clear,
We were once again together, to roam no more,
And who dared suggest it would be shown the door!
With the family around us for a year or two,
We met together often, finding this and that, to do,
And then all of a sudden, children and parents, intent
On seeing foreign life styles into Africa's heartland went!
Would we see them again, was the thought in our mind,
When they boarded that plane to leave us behind,
But we need not have fretted for they promptly returned
Two years later, when their leave had been earned!
Two years later still, it was five who came, not four,
An addition, and for grandparents, a thrill!

Claude Knight

Fifties Bathroom Scales

My young brother and myself
When we were still at school
Though not possessed of wealth
Decided flying transport, ruled.

An advert *Fly to Royal Welsh*
Our theory put to test
Took our savings off the shelf
Booked a flight to Haverfordwest.

On a dampish sort of day
Train and bus to Cardiff Rhoose
In wellingtons made our way
To weigh in on bathroom scales, a ruse.

The cabin and cockpit were one
Six of us, sat there for the ride
Over the coast turbulance was fun
Losing one's inside.

Soon bounced down at Withybush
The taxi then broke down
Just as well we were in no rush
Walked the last stretch to show ground.

We decided, flying was hard upon the feet
After plodding 'round the show
Wearing wellingtons in the heat
Being, the only ones in Pembrokeshire, a mackintosh in tow.

Withybush was basic, turkeys fattening in the tower
They didn't need to weigh us
Back to Rhoose in half an hour.

Taxi was too dear, walked until we caught Western Welsh
Didn't save any time, but we enjoyed ourselves.

Alf Jones

Fancy Free

Living in the Fifties
Was really great for me,
I was young - so full of life
And also fancy free,
I loved to go out dancing
To see who I could meet,
Life was so exciting
The cinema a treat.

Doris Day was beautiful
I loved to hear her sing,
Nat King Cole - he made me swoon
Much more than dear old Bing!
I also felt I was in love
With gorgeous Gregory Peck,
He was really handsome
I wish we could have met.

Pencil skirts with high heeled shoes
I felt I looked so smart,
Every Sunday afternoon
We'd stroll into the park
But time goes by so quickly
The Fifties left behind,
Every year I grow up more
Another life I find.

Hazel M Foster

The Fifties - Remembered

When the Fifties came upon us
I failed my eleven plus,
And was trundled off to *Secondary*
In a Vintage yellow bus.
But in a haze of happy day dreams
My teenage years rolled by,
Guy Mitchell was my hero
And Johnny Ray would cry.
Leaving school I found employment
In a job I did not like,
I travelled to and from it
On my auntie's rusty bike.

But oh, those frivolous fifties,
What memories they bring back.
Weekends we rode the steam train
And played *skiffle* coming back.

The boys wore *drainpipe* trousers
And bright florescent socks,
While girls wore twenty petticoats
Beneath their knee length frocks.

Yes, oh those frivolous fifties
Those halcyon days when young;
Bill Hayley and his Comets
And the songs that Elvis sung.

And soon I found a boyfriend
My hero, what a man!
His mode of transport trendy -
An old blue Austin van.
We met up in the springtime in nineteen fifty nine,
And in autumn we decided I was his and he was mine.

Caroline Shore

Post-War Baby

I was a post-war baby
Just learning how to walk,
As the fifties hauled anchor from the Second World War
The days of ration books
And dripping on bread
The cold war blossomed was it something I said.

I remember the day
When I first started school
It was like walking past Christmas to a very bad dream,
Mothers kissed children
Who were left unawares
In faces wearing masks from the last Halloween.

The radio inhabited
Our everyday life
Till the voice in the box gave way to a dream,
The black and white telly
Brought the stars in our home
And Muffin the Mule brought finesse to the screen.

As the seventy eight's crackled
On our old gramophone
A sound invaded Britain with a curious drone,
Elvis may have captured
The voice in his soul
But I never could remember that sweet rock and roll.

Strange how a memory
Can linger on sport
I can still see Stanley Mathews in his old baggy shorts.

My sands in the hour glass
May sometimes be vague
Still I trundled through the fifties as a proud post-war babe.

David Bridgewater

Fifteen to Eighteen

Ruined landmark on landscapes of education,
With growing concerns appeared recommendations.
Crowther's report, 1959; *Fifteen to Eighteen*,
Emphasising various deficiencies.
In the light of Butler's tripartite system,
A review of secondary education:

School leaving age raised to sixteen,
Sixth form college and technical training,
Organsiation of schools, supplies of teachers,
Quality of their qualifications, training and wages.

Although Butler envisaged these measures,
Their implementation essential, regarded Crowther,
Without *Fifteen to Eighteen* difficult to comprehend change,
Gradually sprouting, not blooming straight away.
His Fifties contribution
Shaped education.
Highlighting deficiencies:
Fifteen to Eighteen.

Soman Balan

An American Throne

This white throne is *reserved*,
even though empty -
there is an old man
who seeks a seat . . .
yet this seat carries a reservation,
it is for the white only,
the old man must wait,
he must stand and wait for a vacant
seat for the black only.
He has human rights
and so sits down,
he sits on the white throne,
yet this throne is *reserved*,
even though empty,
so he is taken,
punished . . .
this old man needs a seat,
yet this seat is *reserved* for the sacred white skin -
a white seat for a white man,
a black seat for a black man.
These white men are in a grey world,
yet these white men rule,
and so this white throne,
this sacred white seat
stays
reserved.

D A Lowe

The Fifties

What a beginning
To nineteen fifty one.
Festival of Britain.
A marriage just begun.

First of September,
Honeymoon in Wales.
Hand sewn dresses,
Shoes in the sales.

Lots of council houses.
Counting up the points.
Just a few shillings
For Sunday joints.

No easy washing,
Just a wooden wringer.
Most of the sewing,
Done with a Singer.

Then the joys of motherhood.
Lovely little boy.
Realisation!
It's not a toy.

What a busy time we had.
Nothing did we shirk,
Fun was the fifties.
Hard was the work.

Rosemary J Povey

Rock Baby Rock

Rock, baby, rock,
Roll, baby, roll,
Bop to me close
Then swing away, doll,
Spin away, spin,
Under my arm,
Then rock ever closer,
Lively and warm.

Roll, baby, roll,
Tossing you on high,
My hands on your waist,
My hands on your thigh,
You swing through my legs
And up with the beat,
You're over my shoulder
And sliding to your feet.

Rock, baby, rock,
Your petticoats a-twirl,
Full skirt flying,
Pony tail a-whirl,
Tight blue jeans
Skinny and new,
Blue suede shoes
Rocking with you.

Esme Francis

Nostalgia

I sat down to listen to my old LP's
Then I put on some old seventy eight's,
Nostalgia crept over me as I closed my eyes
Then drifting back to the time in our lives,
Remembering the gang, the dancing, the dates.

Saturdays we collected the tickets for the dance.
We would then buy some records and sit in a trance
As we played the top bands with rhythm sweet and low.
The sound of Joe Loss, The Squadronaires, and Geraldo.
Lita Rosa, Dennis Lotus, Eve Boswell, they were there,
The harmony and vocalising filled the air.

Excitement at the dance wondering who I would meet.
Then as the band struck up we would start to tap our feet.
Jiving and bopping what great times we had,
Knowing it's gone for ever makes me feel a little sad.

The thrill when the big bands arrived on the scene,
With saxophones, trumpets, and trombones all a-gleam.
We would gather around enthralled when they played,
The wonderful music that those instruments made.
Time now to get back, to the present day
Until once again my old records I will play.

Pamela M Dean

Sandy Socks and Sticks of Rock

On one fine day each year, our holiday was planned
No hotel stay, but just one day, in Blackpool pleasure land
Mum would pack a shopping bag, essentials we would need
Chopped egg butties, custard creams, baby's bottled feed
Plastic sandals, cossies, spades, buckets fishing net
Towels, nappies, facecloth, more clothes should we get wet.

Each child fit to travel, all dressed up spick and span
New bonnet on the baby and parasol on pram
Then off to Preston Station, where trains still ran on steam
Waiting on the platform, mum would count her team
One adult and eight kiddies, the tickets fell one short
But who would spot a tiny tot, a risk she had to court.

And as the journey passed along on sound and rhythm train
Arriving now at Blackpool, my mum would count again
So hand in hand, down to the sand and frolics in the sea
We'd eat butties mum had made, she'd buy a cup of tea
Then clutching on to sixpence, we would run towards the tide
Part of the game, to choose the name, of donkey each would ride.

But sixpence left still in her hand, each year mum was bound
To find one lamb who'd gone astray in children lost and found
All towel dried, but salty skinned, with faces turning brown
We'd feast on chips and candy floss, before the sun went down
With sandy socks and sticks of rock, we'd board the Preston train
A curtained carriage of our own, we'd journey home again.

Sliding gently track to track, the night's air, perfumed steam
All sleepy heads, in need of beds;
Were rocked in childhood dreams.

Angela Mary Thompson

118

Recollections

As I sit here upon the window seat
The sunlight playing on my upturned face
My memory returns to days I keep
Tucked away in mind's most special place.
In the fifties I was in my teens
A precious time of sweet discovery
Not young nor old but somewhere in between
Days when life was still a mystery.
Threepence bought a bag of scraps and chips
Sherbert . . . Jellybabies . . . Liquorice sticks
Lemondade powder with lolly dip
Three ice lollies licked before they dripped.
Scrumping was the biggest lark of all
Over fences for the choosiest pears
It was so exciting I recall
Everyday we tried another dare.
Steam trains puffed below us on the bridge
Standing in the steam was quite a laugh
We knew the penalty but still we did
It getting faces black cost us a bath.
We loved to while away the summer days
Fantasising about who we'd be
It was only dreams that go away
You'd never think it if you looked at me
Those were the days the fifties they were fun
We enjoyed ourselves no matter what
I turn away from the heat of the sun
And place my past where it is not forgot . . .

Sonia Santina

Outside Your Own Front Door

Oh to go back just once more
      and do the things we did
In those days of yesteryear
      when I was just a kid.

I'd give anything to see
      a bunch of sticky-lice
Burst a bubble in the tar
      or suck a lolly-ice.

To play a game of *jinks* again
      or maybe *kick the can*
Then make a winter-warmer
      an' get clouted by me mam.

I could chalk a hopscotch on the side
      an' master top and whip
Play *ellalio* with the gang
      I'd even learn to skip.

To see the corner shop once more
      an' take the bottles back
Play *cowies* with our kid again
      an' wear me long blue mac'.

I'd whizz with my *cheese cutter*
      an' I'd play hangman's knot
And maybe call those words again
      I'm *comin'*, ready or not.

I'd give so much to take a trip
      on the old New Brighton boat
To think of a *tram* an' my ol' mam
      puts a lump inside my throat.

Oh let me spend a little time
        upon a lamppost swing
Or look down grids outside the shops
        with my magnet on a string.

I'd tell those old-time jokes again
        all about *Pat an' Mick*
I'd play a game of marbles
        or maybe off-ground tick.

I'd while away the time again
        with that gang of mine
Cinnamon-sticks; goin' to the *flicks*
        an' laughin' all the time.

Ollie-holes an' leapfrog
        climbin' backyard walls
'Be out after me tea,' you'd say
        when your old mother calls.

One o'learly - two o'leary . . . who could want for more?
Oh for those far-off days again outside your own front door . . .

Norman Whittle

Denim was Strictly for Work

Yes, I remember the fifties.
I was still a teenager then.
All the girls wore dresses
and at eighteen, boys were men.
Conscripted to National Service
for two years, and sometimes more.
Everyone had a choice of jobs,
less incentive to break the law.
The age of the New Look was born
with skirts almost down to the ground.
Radios bounced the music
of the wonderful Big Band sound.
Yes, I remember the Fifties.
People had time to talk.
Girls wore flouncy dresses
and denim was strictly for work.

Mavis Fox

The Invisible Exports

Vivat Regina: on this your glorious Coronation Day.
Everest is conquered by Sir Edmund Hillary.
Your reign is doubly marked today.
While your loyal subjects kneel to obey
Elizabeth, Defender of the Faith, their Liege Sovereign,
Your trusted Whitehall ministers have given
Away Testaments, chocolates and plastic, crested, mugs
To your good children, who sit at tressle tables
Under coloured bunting hanging from the gables.
They drink delicious, orange squash, poured from sparkling jugs,
Enjoying their additional school holiday.
But: all along the quayside, waiting for the morning tide,
At anchor, orphans and young offenders ride,
Aboard a fleet of unmarked Blackbirders,
Slaves for Merino herders,
Ravenous sharks, circling in Botany Bay.
Eager for young, nubile, flesh,
Scenting their prey, they flail and thresh
Under the groaning overhead cargo net.
Live exports thrive, as crime falls like the London rain,
Tears for the innocent, uprooted in a tidal wave of pain,
Littering broken bodies through the outback. We forget
This deep, dark, secret never to be told:
For, it might mar a halcyon day, cloaked in ermine and gold.

Jan Ferrierr

Memories of the Nineteen Fifties

Back in the Fifties I loved Gourock Town
From Larkfield scheme we'd all walk down,
We'd sometimes go fishing at Cardwell Bay
We'd never catch much but stayed there all day.
We went to the baths at the Battery Park
Though I couldn't swim I went for a lark
One day in the water we were all clowning
It's the nearest in my life I came to drowning.
Some days we would walk right round the cloch
Where over the Clyde you'd see Holy Loch,
The man in the lighthouse came out for a chat
Though it's long ago I still recall that
We'd collect empty bottles to pay for our treats
Like going to the pictures or just buying sweets,
Sometimes we'd go camping at Lunderston Bay
We stayed all the weekend and came home on Sunday.
We'd go and pick chestnuts at Sir Guy's Estate
And though it was wrong we climbed over the gate,
We'd walk to the beach at quiet Inverkip
And if it was warm go in for a dip,
Yes, the Fifties they hold some memories for me
Though we were poor we were young and free
For nowadays life is lived far too fast
Though standards are better there was fun in the past

David Wilson

Middle Aged Memories

Remember the Fifties my dears?
Remember our teenage years?
Pat Boone ballads, Nat King Cole,
Yes and the birth of Rock and Roll.
When we wore ponytails, velvet at our throat
And miles of net on our petticoat.
It's sad recalling how some girls cried
When the news came through James Dean had died.

Boys wore drainpipe suits with a velvet collar
And crepe sole shoes was the fashion to follow,
But completing the craze each Edwardian guy
Was never without his slim Jim tie.
Those days of skiffle - so alive,
The coffee bars and the old hand-jive.
Our youth was the Fifties of yesteryear -
But it's us who are in the fifties *now* my dear!

Jean Stewart

Living in the Fifties

Our black and white TV with a very small screen,
Encased in a cabinet just had to be seen.
BBC 1 was the first on cue,
Then ITV brought more programmes to view.
The Festival of Britain in fifty one,
Then the Coronation in fifty three,
Were the events of a lifetime for all to see,
Pop songs began to give us a thrill,
Cliff, Elvis, or Buddy Holly topped the bill.
We sang along with them all
And loved those hits of rock 'n' roll,
Songs that made us happy all day
Sent people whistling at work or play.
Musicals and Westerns brought long cinema queues,
Doris Day or Marilyn Monroe never gave you the blues.
National Service kept young men smart,
Those boys in uniform stole many a heart,
A holiday abroad was something new
An experience shared by just a few
A new generation begun to discover Mars,
As Sputniks One and Two raced off to the stars,
The Atom Bomb brought the nuclear age,
Filling mens' hearts with fear and rage,
An affluent society had just begun,
Cars, radios, transistors all made life more fun.
World War II was becoming a memory
As people shared more prosperity.

Barbara Colman

A Mirror of the Fifties

The fifties opened with Zeal and Zest,
Hilary and Tensing conquered Everest,
Rock 'n' Roll came on the scene,
The greatest music ever seen.

Elvis was born to be Rock's King,
With many disciples following him,
Young and old rocked the nights away,
Swinging bands to bop and sway.

For Stanley Mathews' Blackpool team,
To lift the FA Cup was their dream,
Bolton Wanderers they had to overcome,
Stan's lads' fourth goal finally won.

The Epsom Derby was the jockeys prime race,
Thoroughbred horses could show their pace,
Top jockey Gordon Richards' dream came true,
He finally won the Derby too.

A new horizon in Athletics was born,
Could the four minute mile curtain be torn,
Many said four minutes would never be beaten,
After Roger Bannister words were chewed and eaten.

Ration books were about to pass,
Would there be a new world order here at last,
A cold war of a different kind,
Was about to plague all Mankind.

Towards the end of this decade,
Would hate and avarice begin to fade,
Could a more rewarding challenge at last be waged,
As Sputnik announced Man's Great Space Age.

Jim Wilson

Revival

The truth not easy to believe. Was it really a decade,
Since war came, with fear, misery, hardship and sacrifices made?
In spite of the devastation, folk considered it had been worthwhile.
Could the bereaved and disabled face the 1950's with a smile?
A new outlook, an improved world without mistakes of the past.
Would this promised way of living, be acceptable and last!

Service men and women, demobbed, welcomed home, families
united again.
More supplies, the end of rationing, meant less stress and strain.
Bombed sites were cleared, rebuilding proceeded at a steady pace,
Former slum areas had flats, housing or offices in their place.
Old and new interests enjoyed. Also plans by some were made,
For careers with success and prosperity, so hopefully foundations
laid.

In sport, theatres, cinemas, outstanding success and records
achieved,
Together with radio and television, recognition, awards and
medals received.
Wonderful world-wide scientific and medical discoveries were made.
Clever operations, treatments and cures, given deserved honour
and accolade.
New songs and dances, tenpin bowling, created a lively scene,
Bringing enjoyment, and light heartedness, for a long time not seen.

In '45 our boarding and breeding kennels had been tentatively
founded,
By its popularity and success, both of us were really astounded.
Exhibiting our Dalmatians at dog shows, brought enjoyment and
pleasure,
Also new friendships. The hard work, long hours, never thought
to measure.
The birth of our daughter made the family circle happily complete,
in her games, she had four-legged playmates eager to compete.

Left a Kentish suburb, for a village and rural life - quite new.
Added budgies, canaries, poultry, cats and rabbits - our
menagerie grew.
Learnt about, became accustomed to, many wildlife birds and
creatures,
Endured the rigours of winter, snowed-in, isolated, just regular
features.
Meanwhile the future appeared hopeful, as trade and commerce
boomed.
Would this country enjoy prosperity, as the 1960's decade loomed?

Ethel L Thake

Demolition

It's time to leave our old house
The bugs will no longer bite
The candles put out for ever
We'll have electricity for light.

No more sharing our big bed
A room for each, we'll have instead.
No more overcoats, to keep us warm
Mam's bought blankets, clean but torn.

No lamppost outside the front door
Knotted rope that makes our hands sore.
We'll have a garden
But what's one of them.

Where will we play hop skotch
Can we have a den.
No more dirty entries
Full of Bogey men.

Who'll go the errands
For her at number ten.
What about my cleaning job
Three sets of steps a tanner.

I can't go
Mam won't let me stay
No one wants to help me
As my life's being packed away

I'm not that important
No one hears what I say.
I promise house
That I'll be back
One day.

Emma Shaw

Thanks to Nasser!

The Suez Crisis stole the news
In nineteen-fifty-six,
When Nasser and the old canal
Put Eden in a fix!
In spite of all that worldly strife,
What I remember best
Was petrol rationing coming back,
And you need not take a test!

They let you function on your own
Without a licence holder,
Which gave you bags of confidence
And made you feel much bolder.
The test came back, I passed with ease,
And all my skies were blue.
And I always thank old Nasser
For helping me get through!

Eric Rosser

The Turning of a History's Page - 6th February 1952

The day started as would any other
With mundane tasks oh! so pressing,
Time checks given by vigilant mother.
Bus would be missed if too much lagging.
Arrived in time to sign in before the bell,
Young head full of dreams of doings after five
Nothing different as day was passing could I tell
Loud speaker sounds *Attention! Attention!*
Normality to rive,
We listen casually, unsuspecting without foreboding,
'The King is Dead,' with reverence it is said,
Shock!, Horror! Time turns to stone
Our senses chilling,
Unable to grasp lost to us our beloved figurehead,
Silence remains, everyone focuses
On memories personal,
Our dear King's pictorial life through mind's eye pass.
Sharers were we at state and family occasions.
Through camera's flash.
Senses from shock to normality returning,
We hear the words *Long live the Queen*
A page of history we bore witness to the turning,
Subjects silent grief and shock all go to say
to us all you a good King have been.

Margaret M Walker

The Weekend Treat Shop

Behind the bottle bottomed glass in the windows,
Great gleaming jars stood in tight and tidy rows,
Filled to the top with tummy-tempting sweets,
Taunting and teasing us to stop and buy and eat.

Round red aniseed balls were eight for a penny,
Though two for a farthing didn't seem very many,
Chocolate bars cost the princely sum of thruppence,
But chewing gum could be bought for only tuppence.

In boxes on the counter, just inside the doors,
Sherbert dabs were sold with thick liquorice straws,
Bright penny gobstoppers, twice as big as your eyes,
Ha'penny ones never seemed to be half their size!

Penny chews - tasting of raspberry, cherry, lemon,
And salad bowls popping us straight to seventh heaven.
Those chewy brown toffee nuts and sticky honeycomb
Made mouth-watering memories on the journey home.

The multicoloured jellies and super candy fags,
Mixed with rose coloured berries in rustling paper bags.
Unforgotten favourites I still like to munch
Pineapple cubes, murray mints and scrumptious toffee crunch.

Sometimes on a Sunday, for an unexpected treat,
Dad stopped by the shop for some more expensive sweets:
Quality Street, Melba Fruits; or if some took his fancy
A super box of Callard and Bowsers Chocolate Candy.

Janis Priestley

Hero

He died young, Georgie.
Back in the '50's I think.
After he joined the army and
kissed us all goodbye.

His smile flashed whiter
that day when, bright
Against sun burnt skin
His gypsy curls carelessly
tumbled; dark of hair and eye.

We could not live without him!
But he promised amid tears
He'd remember and be back
Before we girls had grown.

Years passed. I saw him.
Old and utterly charmless,
bloated with discontent.
The youth had died in Georgie.
Now in his 50's I think.

Valerie Curtis